21st
Century
Skills Library

COOL SCIENCE CAREERS

VIRTUAL REALITY SPECIALIST

KELLY MILNER HALLS

Published in the United States of America by
Cherry Lake Publishing, Ann Arbor, Michigan
www.cherrylakepublishing.com

Content Adviser
Robert Pastel, Professor of Computer Science, Michigan Technological University

Credits
Photos: Cover and page 1, ©AP Photo/Shizuo Kambayashi; page 4, ©AP Photo/
Michael Schmelling; page 7, ©Adams Picture Library t/a apl/Alamy; page 8,
©doug steley/Alamy; page 9, ©Content Mine International/Alamy; page 10,
©Frances Roberts/Alamy; page 13, ©67photo/Alamy; page 15, ©AP Photo/Luca
Bruno; page 17, ©AP Photo/Eckehard Schulz, File; page 18, ©AP Photo/Oded
Balilty; page 21, ©David J. Green - Lifestyle/Alamy; page 23, ©Blend Images/Alamy;
page 24, ©AP Photo/Tina Fineberg; page 26, ©Katya Palladina/Alamy; page 27,
©AP Photo/Ted S. Warren; page 28, ©AP Photo/Koji Sasahara

Library of Congress Cataloging-in-Publication Data
Halls, Kelly Milner, 1957–
  Virtual reality specialist / by Kelly Milner Halls.
      p. cm.—(Cool science careers)
  Includes index.
  ISBN-13: 978-1-60279-503-7
  ISBN-10: 1-60279-503-7
  1. Human—computer interaction—Vocational guidance—Juvenile literature.
  2. Virtual reality—Vocational guidance—Juvenile literature. 3. Computer
software developers—Juvenile literature. 4. Computer engineers—Juvenile
literature. I. Title. II. Series.
  QA76.9.H85H346 2010
  004.01'9—dc22   2008046011

Cherry Lake Publishing would like to acknowledge
the work of The Partnership for 21st Century Skills.
Please visit *www.21stcenturyskills.org* for more information.

TABLE OF CONTENTS

CHAPTER ONE
IN THE BEGINNING

Have you ever shrunk yourself to explore how the bloodstream works from the inside? Have you ever rocketed to Mars to study its red, rocky soil?

Douglas Engelbart was an engineer who played a key role in developing computer technology.

Unless you're writing a fiction essay, the answer to each of these questions is NO! So far, these journeys are impossible. But **virtual** reality specialists are working to make these activities possible.

Experts called virtual reality specialists use the magic of computer technology. They can create imaginary places called simulated environments. With special goggles and other hardware, real people can step into these make-believe worlds. It's as if they have stepped into a movie or a video game.

It all started in 1962 with an electrical engineer named Douglas Engelbart. He was a radar expert in World War II (1939–1945). He understood that computers could help people see real things represented by images on electronic screens. For example, airplanes or submarines on radar screens don't look like airplanes or submarines. They are displayed as tiny blips of light. But the person reading the image knows that they are real airplanes or submarines.

Engelbart dreamed of making the world a better place by taking that concept even further. He took a job at Stanford Research Institute. His goal was to explore how computers could add to human intelligence.

Engelbart made important discoveries. He created important digital libraries, books full of information saved on computers rather than paper. He also invented the computer mouse. If a person moved and clicked the mouse, a cursor on the computer screen responded. A bridge was created between man and machine. The door to virtual reality was opened, just a little, and people waited for others to widen the crack.

Ivan Sutherland was ready. In 1962, Sutherland invented the light pen, a device that can be used to select objects on a computer screen. A short time later, Sutherland developed Sketchpad. It was a program that allowed people to create images on the computer screen.

LEARNING & INNOVATION SKILLS

Stereoscopy was invented by Sir Charles Wheatstone in 1838. It tricked the human eye. How? By making it merge two photos viewed side by side into a single three-dimensional (3-D) image. William Gruber took the stereoscope a step further. He introduced the View-Master at the 1939 New York World's Fair. This invention reduced photographs to tiny slides and placed them in a circle on a disk. You could look at the pictures through a special viewer. Gruber's invention was meant to replace postcards with a fun, 3-D twist. It became a kid-friendly introduction to virtual reality that has been popular ever since.

The View-Master stereoscope was one of the earliest virtual reality devices.

A third inventor, Morton Heilig, also made an important contribution in 1962. He patented the Sensorama that year, though it was actually created in 1957. The Sensorama combined sights, sounds, scents, and even physical feelings to simulate the human experience in 3-D.

Elements of all three of these virtual reality specialists' creations were combined in the 1970s. It was a recipe for

A pilot trainee sits inside a flight simulator.

Jurassic Park's *special effects helped make it one of the most successful movies in Hollywood history.*

magic. Pilots could soon practice flying jets on flight simulators. They could gain experience without putting passengers or people on the ground at risk.

It was Hollywood that took the next giant step. In the late 1970s, computers helped bring space into focus in *Star Wars*. In 1993, computers helped dinosaurs spring back to life in the motion picture *Jurassic Park*. The video gaming industry followed Hollywood's lead. Virtual reality became the wave of the future.

CHAPTER TWO
ON THE JOB

What exactly do virtual reality specialists do? They combine math, art, computer science, and engineering skills to make the unreal seem real. They use technology to build bridges between computers and human beings.

Millions of video gamers have played in the virtual world of The Sims.

According to author Michael Heim, there are many kinds of virtual reality bridges. If you've ever played *The Sims*, you've experienced **simulation**—a virtual imitation of real life. By combining computer programs, story lines, and animation, a new "world" is created and controlled by the gamer. People all over the world enjoy the careful design and planning that went into *The Sims*.

21ˢᵀ CENTURY CONTENT

Do you think there are enough young girls interested in science? How about girls that actually become scientists when they grow up? Encouraging young girls to pursue careers in science, math, and technology is still an issue in the 21st century. Take the video gaming industry as an example. Many girls and women like to play video games. But there are fewer women behind the scenes, developing those games and all of their cool features. Having more female workers in the video game industry is important in many ways. For example, it could lead to the creation of games that appeal to even more consumers.

World of Warcraft is a very successful example of **artificiality**. It is a virtual world that's different from what we consider ordinary. Virtual reality specialists create fictional worlds filled with virtual life-forms. But instead of controlling the worlds, as they do in simulations, participants step into the virtual worlds. It's artificial but real at the same time.

LEARNING & INNOVATION SKILLS

Mastering a second language after years of speaking only one can be difficult. Full immersion (speaking only the new language) is the best way to learn. But how can you speak only German if you live in California? A trip to Realtown may soon be the perfect solution.

An international team of professors from Mexico and Jordan used Swedish software to create a virtual reality community. Realtown was the result of their teamwork. Now students can take virtual trips to banks, grocery stores, and other ordinary places where the language they are studying is spoken. Realtown makes it easy for students to practice their new language skills from the comfort of a classroom or home computer station.

The flight computers found in modern bomber planes are very important to military operations.

Virtual reality specialists use **interaction** to blend human effort with computer programs. This is sometimes used to help people learn new facts. Medical students at the University of Leicester in the United Kingdom work with a virtual **autopsy** program. They are able to learn about the human body without ever touching one.

Have you ever put on a special helmet or goggles to see more than you normally see? Then you've experienced **immersion**. Special eyepieces in the goggles called Head Mounted Displays (HMDs) project the images seen through the goggles. Firefighters see the floor plans of burning buildings to help rescue survivors. Fighter pilots see their bombing targets from miles above the ground. DisneyQuest visitors can fight theme park pirates or study dinosaurs as if they weren't extinct.

21ST CENTURY CONTENT

CyberWorld, Inc., in Ontario, Canada, is one leading virtual reality company. Virtual reality specialists at CyberWorld create software for clients who want to simulate real experiences. SeaWorld, for example, asked them to take people on an underwater adventure without ever getting wet. The Canadian Department of National Defence spent $300 million to have CyberWorld develop special software. Now they can train their soldiers without spilling a single drop of blood.

Companies such as CyberWorld are blazing new trails. They prove that with imagination and hard work, almost anything is possible in the realm of virtual reality.

Telepresence is another product made possible by virtual reality specialists. All you need is a computer and a webcam to make use of telepresence. These tools allow your image to

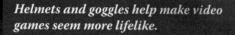
Helmets and goggles help make video games seem more lifelike.

be sent to another computer far away. You can visit with distant friends even if you have to stay close to home.

Full body immersion is like immersion except it makes use of more than goggles. Gloves, bodysuits, and helmets are used to intensify the simulated experience. They seem to carry your whole body into imaginary worlds.

The last bridge is called **network communications**. Network communications makes it possible for many people to share the same experience at roughly the same time. One example is a series of computers connected to one another in an office building. Another is a group of television stations sending images to millions of TVs.

LEARNING & INNOVATION SKILLS

Some specialists work to make virtual reality a useful technology for the world of medicine. Some programs, for example, produce 3-D images of a patient's organs or body parts. These images can then be rotated in different directions. This helps doctors learn more about a patient's problems and prepare themselves for surgery.

In many ways, virtual reality software is a useful problem-solving tool. Being as prepared as possible before any incisions are made helps doctors perform operations successfully. As specialists develop new programs and software— and as the prices of these products decrease— virtual reality may make an even greater impact on medicine.

Online gaming is just one of the ways to make use of network communications.

CHAPTER THREE
EDUCATION AND TRAINING

Are you a deep thinker? Are you a person who sees a problem as a challenge just waiting to be mastered? If you are, then a career as a virtual reality specialist might be right for you.

Virtual reality devices can be used to help people recover from injuries and learn to move normally again.

Does your disabled friend want to try waterskiing, even though he can't stand or walk? Has your grandma always wanted to visit Italy, in spite of her fear of flying? If you can look beyond what they can't do and imagine what is possible, virtual reality wants you.

Almost any work that involves coming up with new inventions is inspired by what goes right *and* what goes wrong. Paying close attention to how your world works and to what doesn't work is great early training.

LIFE & CAREER SKILLS

Most high school students can only prepare for careers as virtual reality specialists by reading or playing games at home. This isn't so for students at East Marshall High School in Le Grand, Iowa. The school received a slightly used $100,000 Fakespace immersive virtual reality system. The donor, the Mayo Clinic and Foundation for Medical Education and Research, also provided expert instruction on how to use it.

Thanks to this generous gift, some students at the school can get a head start on their career training.

LIFE & CAREER SKILLS

Medical experts need to be prepared for unexpected events such as natural disasters or disease epidemics. But how do you train employees to handle events that everyone hopes will never happen? Simulate them! Some hospitals now employ virtual reality specialists. The New York City Health and Hospitals Corporation's simulation specialists earn between $46,000 and $100,000 per year. Their job is to create simulations of catastrophic events. The simulations are used to help prepare doctors, nurses, and other medical staff to deal with disasters.

Study how things are put together and how they come apart. Build a birdhouse or a bookshelf. Does it serve your needs? Can it be improved? Study the questions. Propose possible answers. Take your creation apart, redesign it, and put it back together. Then do it all over again.

Are you a gamer and a fan of electronic devices? That's excellent if you want to be a virtual reality specialist. Play

Studying video games can be a great way to learn about the different ways people can interact with virtual worlds.

every game and use every console and every plug-in extra you can find. Play with joysticks, steering wheels, and oddball controllers. *Guitar Hero* is one of the most popular games to debut in decades. It is also a brilliant example of what a team of virtual reality specialists can do when they set their minds to it.

Do you like math? If you do, it'll come in handy as a virtual reality specialist. Numbers are the key to communicating with computers. They allow people to write the computer programs that open imaginary doors. Math skills are important for every virtual reality specialist.

Are you artistic? Can you picture things in your head and capture them on paper? If you can, you could be a key player on a virtual reality team. You can't design new worlds without picturing them first. A good imagination is essential to being a virtual reality specialist.

If you decide to become a virtual reality specialist, engineering and computer science will be part of your advanced education. Colleges all over the world offer degrees in computer science and engineering. Some offer programs with an emphasis on virtual reality.

Are classes your only way to prepare? The answer is no, thanks to professional internships. These are temporary paid or unpaid jobs for students. Organizations such as Cyber-World, Disney, Microsoft, Bungie, EA Games, and the United States Department of Defense offer internships. Students can learn while working in the field they hope to enter after graduation. Internships can help you get to know people already working as virtual reality specialists.

Pay close attention in math class if you want to become a virtual reality specialist.

CHAPTER FOUR
THE NEXT LEVEL

Virtual reality is at the leading edge of technology. But even **innovators** need to look to the future in order to grow. So what's next for the field of virtual reality?

Video game designer Shigeru Miyamoto demonstrates Wii Fit, *a virtual exercise game for the Nintendo Wii.*

Virtual reality specialists will continue to push the limits of technology. And virtual reality does have limits. For example, the virtual footrace you run—and see through your virtual reality goggles—only feels real until your body hits your actual living room wall. But virtual reality specialists at VirtuSphere have come up with a solution.

Step inside their 8.5-foot (2.6 meter) sphere while wearing those goggles, and your motions will be virtually endless. Picture a hamster inside a clear, plastic play ball. It is able to run in any direction because the ball turns naturally with its movements. The VirtuSphere is just like that play ball, except you're the hamster. Instead of seeing what is outside those clear plastic walls, you're seeing the world created by computer software.

Former VirtuSphere boss Alexey Palladin claims, "If you can put a person inside the sphere and have the sphere rotate, you will have limitless possibilities of traveling in virtual reality."

Experts say the VirtuSphere could be used in video game applications. It would be great in arcades or amusement parks.

The VirtuSphere could be used by gamers or professionals in need of virtual training.

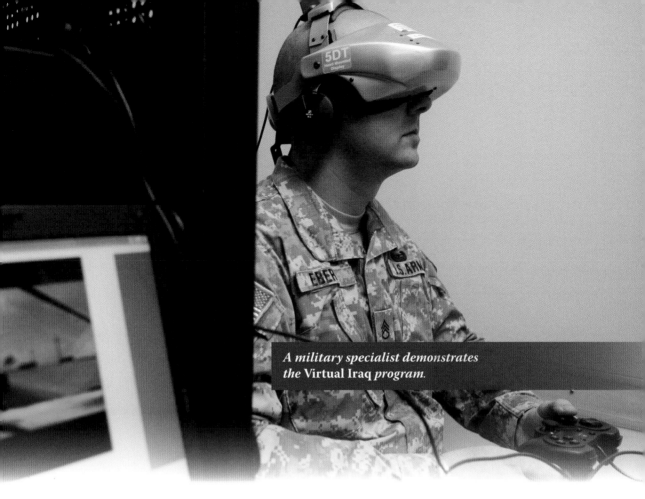

A military specialist demonstrates the Virtual Iraq *program.*

The VirtuSphere could have more practical uses, too. It could help train firefighters or athletes.

Other experts are working on using virtual reality tools in different ways. One application is helping people with mental health issues. *Virtual Iraq* is one example of using virtual reality technology as a mental health tool. It is a simulation of life in a war zone. After exposure to violent battle settings, some troops develop what's known as post-traumatic stress disorder, or PTSD. *Virtual Iraq* helps soldiers work through their painful experiences without setting foot back on foreign soil.

Once again, virtual reality specialists identified a problem and used their imagination and training to solve it. The possibilities in virtual reality are endless. Some experts predict that people will soon be wearing headsets and interacting with computers in 3-D. Many think that virtual reality will become part of regular daily life. Whatever is next for virtual reality, the future just might depend on you!

Some virtual reality specialists are working on technology that allows a user's brain to interact directly with a computer.

SOME FAMOUS VIRTUAL REALITY SPECIALISTS

Douglas Engelbart (1925–) is an American inventor and the forefather of human–computer interaction. He is best known for creating the computer mouse. Problem solving was his primary inspiration.

Morton Heilig (1926–1997) was a filmmaker who created the multimedia experience known as the Sensorama, a device that simulated experiences through sight, sound, touch, and smell. He is often called the Father of Virtual Reality.

Myron Krueger (1942–) is an educator and computer artist. He created a virtual reality system called VIDEOPLACE, in which environments are projected on walls instead of through goggles. His vision was to make art interactive.

Jaron Lanier (1960–) was one of the first computer scientists to use the phrase *virtual reality* in the early 1980s. He founded VPL Research, the first company to sell virtual reality products. He is currently a scholar-in-residence at the University of California, Berkeley.

Howard Rheingold (1947–) is an author who writes and researches technology issues, including virtual reality topics. He wrote one of the best-known books on virtual reality.

Ivan Sutherland (1938–) is an electrical engineer and computer scientist. He invented Sketchpad, a computer program in which a person uses an interactive tablet to draw images on a computer screen.

GLOSSARY

artificiality (ar-tuh-fih-shee-A-luh-tee) a virtual reality application in which people can enter a made-up world

autopsy (AW-top-see) an examination of a dead body to learn more about why or how the person died

full body immersion (FULL BOD-ee i-MUR-zhuhn) a virtual reality experience in which a person wears a helmet, goggles, gloves, and a bodysuit to make it feel as if he or she is actually in another place

immersion (i-MUR-zhuhn) the process of becoming completely involved in something, such as a virtual world

innovators (IN-uh-vay-turz) people who come up with new or different ideas or inventions

interaction (in-tur-ACK-shuhn) action between two or more people or things

network communications (NET-wurk kuh-myoo-nuh-KAY-shunz) using technology to link computers together to allow users to communicate with one another

sedentary (SED-uhn-tair-ee) not physically active

simulation (sim-yuh-LAY-shuhn) an imitation of real-life activity

virtual (VUR-choo-uhl) created or extended by computer software

FOR MORE INFORMATION

BOOKS

Grady, Sean M. *Virtual Reality: Simulating and Enhancing the World with Computers*. New York: Facts on File, 2003.

Wyborny, Sheila. *Virtual Reality*. San Diego: Blackbirch Press, 2003.

Yount, Lisa. *Virtual Reality*. Detroit: Lucent, 2005.

WEB SITES

Virtual Reality: A Short Introduction
www-vrl.umich.edu/intro/
Basic information about virtual reality technology from the University of Michigan's College of Engineering

VirtuSphere
www.virtusphere.com/
Pictures of the VirtuSphere and more information about its uses

INDEX

ABOUT THE AUTHOR

Kelly Milner Halls is the author of 25 books, including innovative nonfiction about dinosaurs, mummies, albino animals, horses, dogs, zoos, and cryptozoology. She lives in Spokane, Washington.